Shadows of Night

Shadows of Night

The Hidden World of the Little Brown Bat

Barbara Bash

Sierra Club Books For Children ▪ San Francisco

The Sierra Club, founded in 1892 by John Muir, has devoted itself to the study
and protection of the earth's scenic and ecological resources — mountains,
wetlands, woodlands, wild shores and rivers, deserts and plains. The publishing
program of the Sierra Club offers books to the public as a nonprofit educational
service in the hope that they may enlarge the public's understanding of the
Club's basic concerns. The Sierra Club has some sixty chapters in the United
States and in Canada. For information about how you may participate in its
programs to preserve wilderness and the quality of life, please address inquiries
to Sierra Club, 730 Polk Street, San Francisco, CA 94109.

FIRST EDITION

Calligraphy by Barbara Bash

Acknowledgments

The author extends special thanks to Patricia Morton at Bat
Conservation International in Austin, Texas; Dr. Elizabeth Kalko
at the National Museum of Natural History in Washington, DC; and
Rick Adams at the University of Colorado in Boulder.

PRINTED IN THE UNITED STATES OF AMERICA

10 9 8 7 6 5 4 3 2 1

In China, the bat is a symbol of
good fortune and wisdom
and is often painted in red,
the color of joy.

This book is dedicated to
the bats of the world —
wondrous creatures of the dark.

The evening sky deepens into night. Birds return to their roosts, and many other animals quietly nestle into their burrows. But some creatures are just waking up. Dark shapes flutter across the sky, suddenly turning, diving, swooping. Bats are beginning to hunt.

This is the story of the Little Brown Bat, one of the most common bats in North America. For its small size, this species has a very long life span — sometimes more than thirty years. Its scientific name is *Myotis lucifugus*. These Latin words mean "mouse-eared" and "light-fleeing."

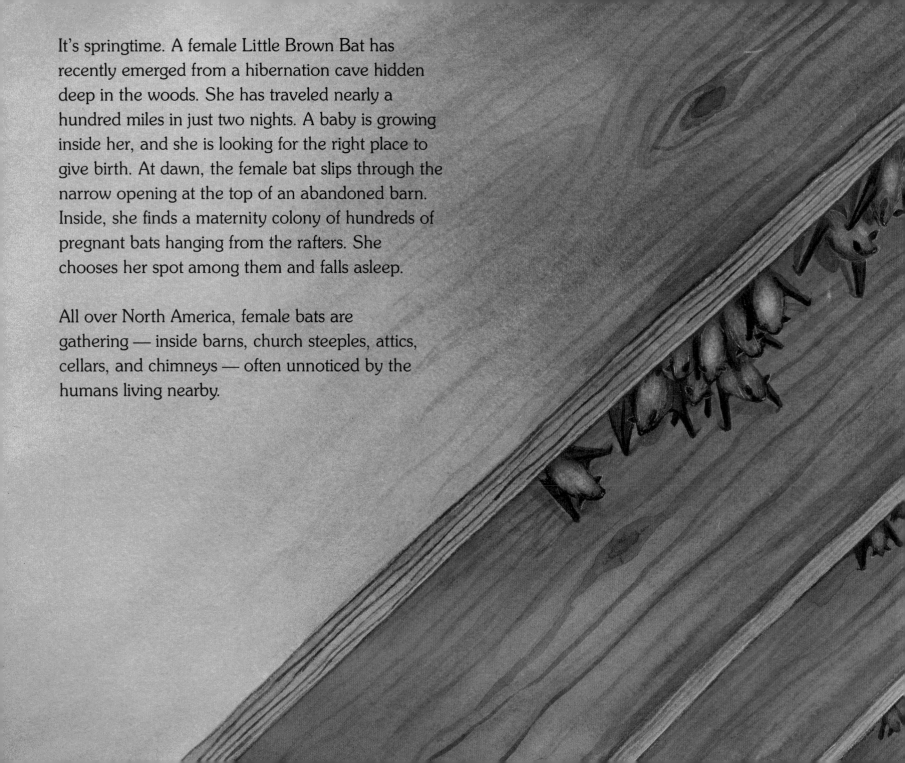

It's springtime. A female Little Brown Bat has recently emerged from a hibernation cave hidden deep in the woods. She has traveled nearly a hundred miles in just two nights. A baby is growing inside her, and she is looking for the right place to give birth. At dawn, the female bat slips through the narrow opening at the top of an abandoned barn. Inside, she finds a maternity colony of hundreds of pregnant bats hanging from the rafters. She chooses her spot among them and falls asleep.

All over North America, female bats are gathering — inside barns, church steeples, attics, cellars, and chimneys — often unnoticed by the humans living nearby.

Two months later, the baby bat is ready to be born. During the birth, the mother turns herself head up (which is upside down for a bat). She hangs from her thumb claws and forms a basket with her tail membrane. The baby is born feet first and clutches immediately for a foothold with its well-developed toes, squirming and pushing to help the rest of its body emerge.

As soon as the baby is born, the mother turns head down again and cradles the baby under her wing to nurse. As it drinks the sweet, warm milk, she cuts the umbilical cord and grooms the baby carefully.

During the first day, the baby bat clings to its mother, snuggled under her wing. Its body is covered with fine, silky hair, and its eyes are still closed. The baby grips its mother's fur tightly to prevent a fall. It also latches on securely to her nipple as it nurses. If the mother is disturbed, she will carry her baby with her as she circles inside the dark barn.

Hundreds of other baby bats (called pups) were born in the barn around the same time. When the mother bats go out to hunt at night, they leave the pups clustered together tightly, hanging from the barn ceiling. Waiting for their mothers to return, they romp and tussle like kittens. To a human, the heat and the dense, pungent smell of a bat roost is overpowering. But to a naked bat pup, the roost is wonderfully warm and comforting.

When a mother returns, she finds her baby in the midst of all the screaming pups by calling out and listening for its particular cry. When she reaches her baby, she sniffs and licks it, making sure it is the right one. Then they settle down to nurse.

In about three weeks, the young bats are ready to fly. Their pink skin is now covered with soft, brown fur, and their wings have grown much larger. The first attempts to fly around the barn are full of confusion. Jostling, squeaking pups are everywhere. One young bat manages to take off and fly to the other side without colliding with the others. But landing is harder. The pup doesn't know how to flip around at the end of its flight, so it lands head up and has to turn around awkwardly on the wall.

By the time they are a month old, the young bats have
stopped nursing and have begun to follow their mothers
out at night, imitating their flight patterns and learning to
hunt. Now the young bats are almost full grown. Their
wingspan is about ten inches, yet their bodies are less than
three inches long. They weigh only a quarter of an
ounce — less than a pencil! Soon they are making quick
rolls, tight turns at top speed, and sideslips in midair.
They will need these skills to catch fast-flying insects.

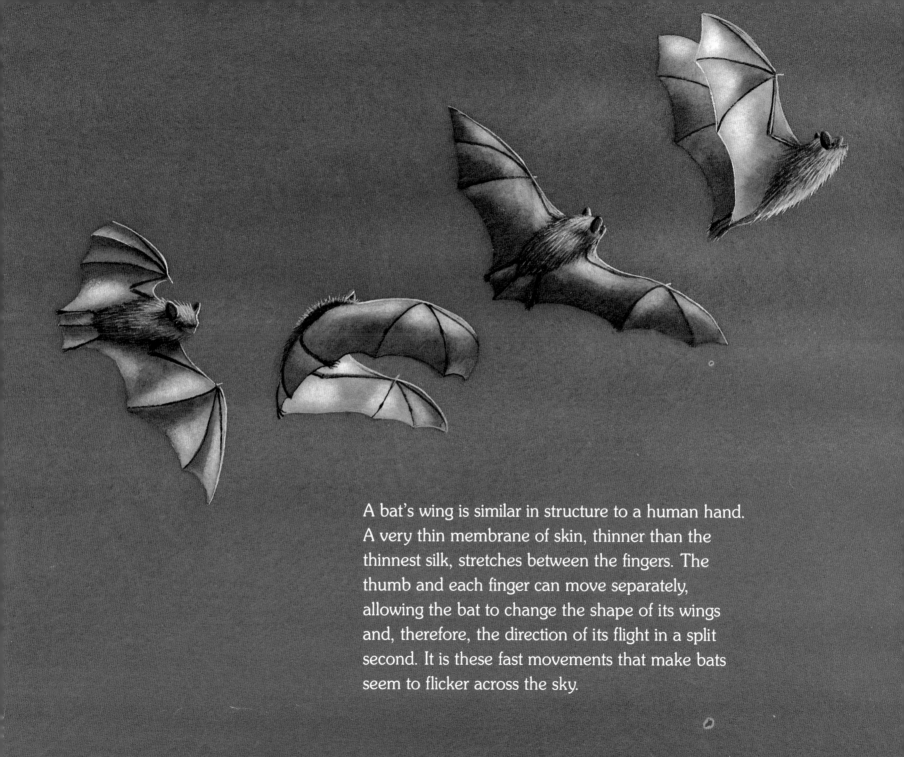

A bat's wing is similar in structure to a human hand. A very thin membrane of skin, thinner than the thinnest silk, stretches between the fingers. The thumb and each finger can move separately, allowing the bat to change the shape of its wings and, therefore, the direction of its flight in a split second. It is these fast movements that make bats seem to flicker across the sky.

Most people think that bats are blind, but Little Brown Bats have eyes that allow them to see in dim light. Much more important is the bat's ability to "see with its ears." As it flies, the bat makes a continuous clicking sound too high-pitched for humans to hear. By listening for the echoes from the clicks, the bat can instantly determine the size, speed, and direction of objects in the dark. This process is called echolocation.

Little Brown Bats use echolocation to hunt for their prey —
moths, mayflies, mosquitoes, and beetles. On summer nights,
bats like to fly over water where insects dart and circle. The bat
scans an area a few yards ahead with sound waves, clicking
about ten times a second. When it swoops in on its prey, the
clicking increases to a ''feeding buzz'' of about two hundred clicks
a second. Then the bat hits the insect with its wing, scoops it up
with its tail membrane, and tosses it into its mouth. In one hour,
a bat can catch more than six hundred bugs!

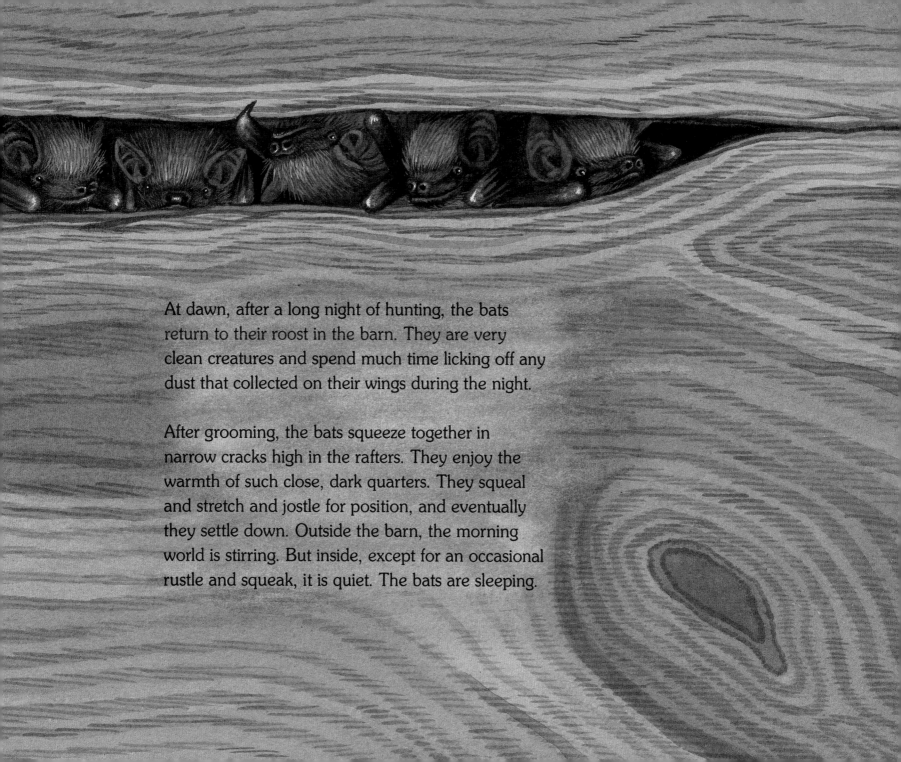

At dawn, after a long night of hunting, the bats
return to their roost in the barn. They are very
clean creatures and spend much time licking off any
dust that collected on their wings during the night.

After grooming, the bats squeeze together in
narrow cracks high in the rafters. They enjoy the
warmth of such close, dark quarters. They squeal
and stretch and jostle for position, and eventually
they settle down. Outside the barn, the morning
world is stirring. But inside, except for an occasional
rustle and squeak, it is quiet. The bats are sleeping.

Late in the summer, Little Brown Bats begin to gather at "bat conventions." Maternity colonies of females and youngsters gradually leave their summer homes and fly to large caves. There they are joined by the males, who have been roosting alone and moving from place to place all summer. Night after night, thousands of bats swarm in and out of the caves. Amid all this confusion, mating takes place, but the babies will not be born until the following summer. First the bats must survive the winter. As the weather cools, clouds of bats begin to travel toward hibernation caves hidden deep in the hills.

During the bat's long winter sleep, its heartbeat slows
from about four hundred beats a minute to under twenty-
five. At the same time, its body temperature falls to just
above freezing. The bat is now in a state called deep
torpor, which allows it to sleep for up to three months
without stirring. While it hibernates, the bat lives off the
fat stored in its body.

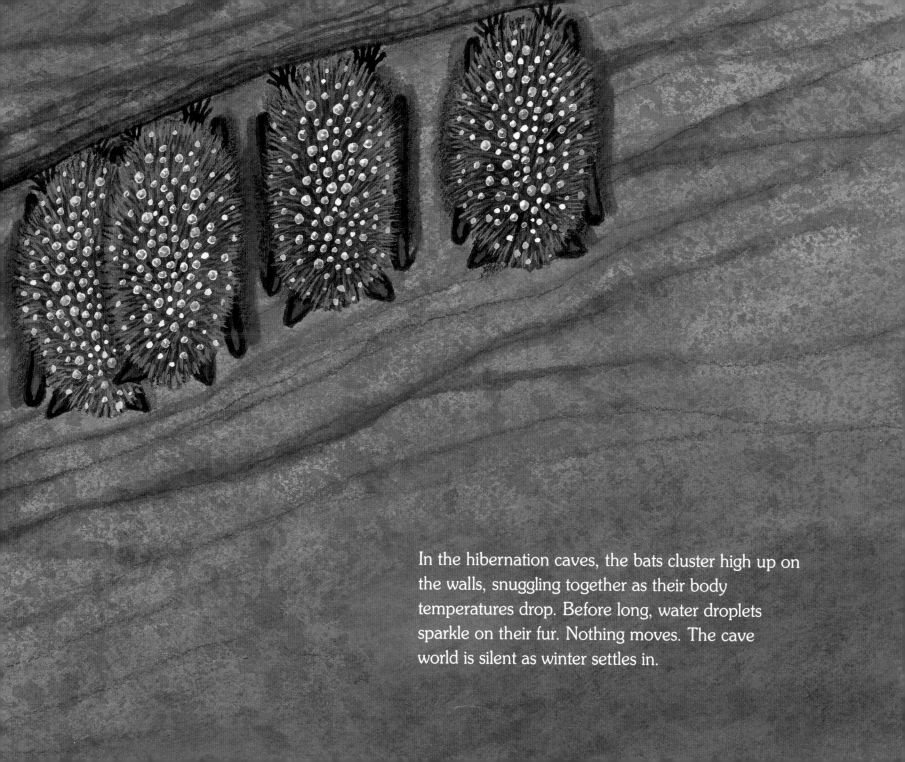

In the hibernation caves, the bats cluster high up on the walls, snuggling together as their body temperatures drop. Before long, water droplets sparkle on their fur. Nothing moves. The cave world is silent as winter settles in.

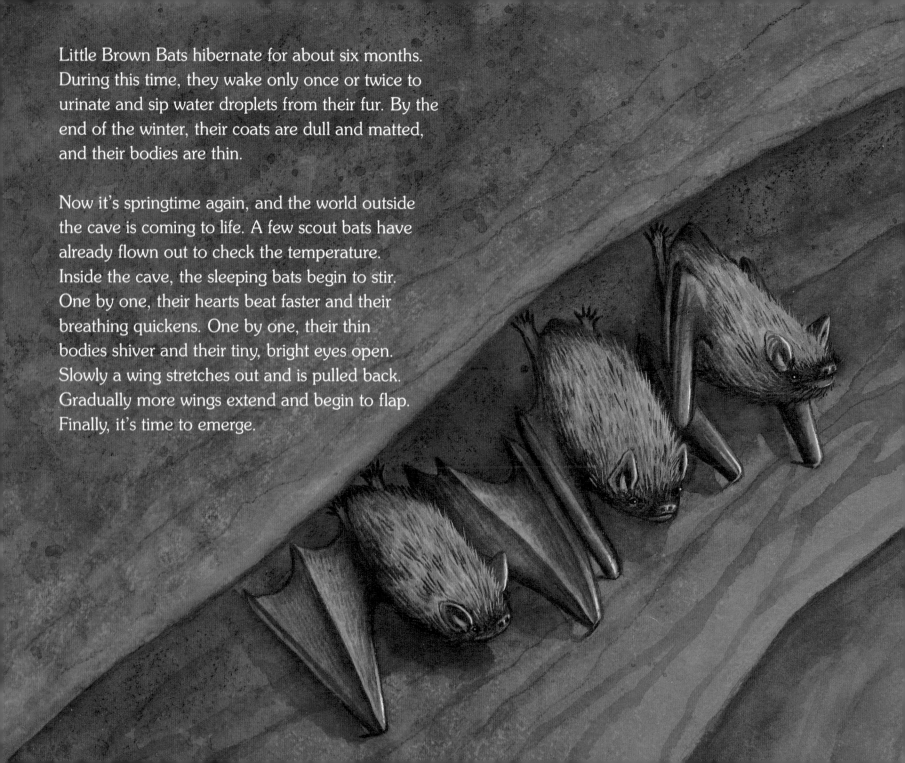

Little Brown Bats hibernate for about six months. During this time, they wake only once or twice to urinate and sip water droplets from their fur. By the end of the winter, their coats are dull and matted, and their bodies are thin.

Now it's springtime again, and the world outside the cave is coming to life. A few scout bats have already flown out to check the temperature. Inside the cave, the sleeping bats begin to stir. One by one, their hearts beat faster and their breathing quickens. One by one, their thin bodies shiver and their tiny, bright eyes open. Slowly a wing stretches out and is pulled back. Gradually more wings extend and begin to flap. Finally, it's time to emerge.

More about Bats

Bats are the only mammals that fly. There are nearly a thousand different kinds of bats in the world. Huge tropical fruit bats (also called flying foxes) navigate by eyesight and eat fruit and flower nectar. They are essential for the pollination and reseeding of many important plants — bananas, cashews, avocados, and figs, to name a few. Many other bats, including the Little Brown Bat, eat vast quantities of insects every night. Some bats even hunt fish and frogs.

Bats are one of the most helpful and fascinating creatures on earth, but because of some people's ignorance and fear, many bats are being destroyed. Throughout the world, bats desperately need our help and protection.

3rd finger
4th finger
5th finger
Tail
2nd finger
Thumb
Forearm

The wings of all bats are structured very much like human hands, with a thumb and four longer fingers. Bats belong to the scientific order *Chiroptera*, which means "hand-wing" in Latin.

Indian Flying Fox
SOUTHEAST ASIA

Bats come in many sizes — from the huge flying fox, with a wingspan of nearly six feet, to the tiny hog-nosed bat, which is no bigger than a bumblebee and weighs less than a penny.

Kitti's Hog-nosed Bat
THAILAND

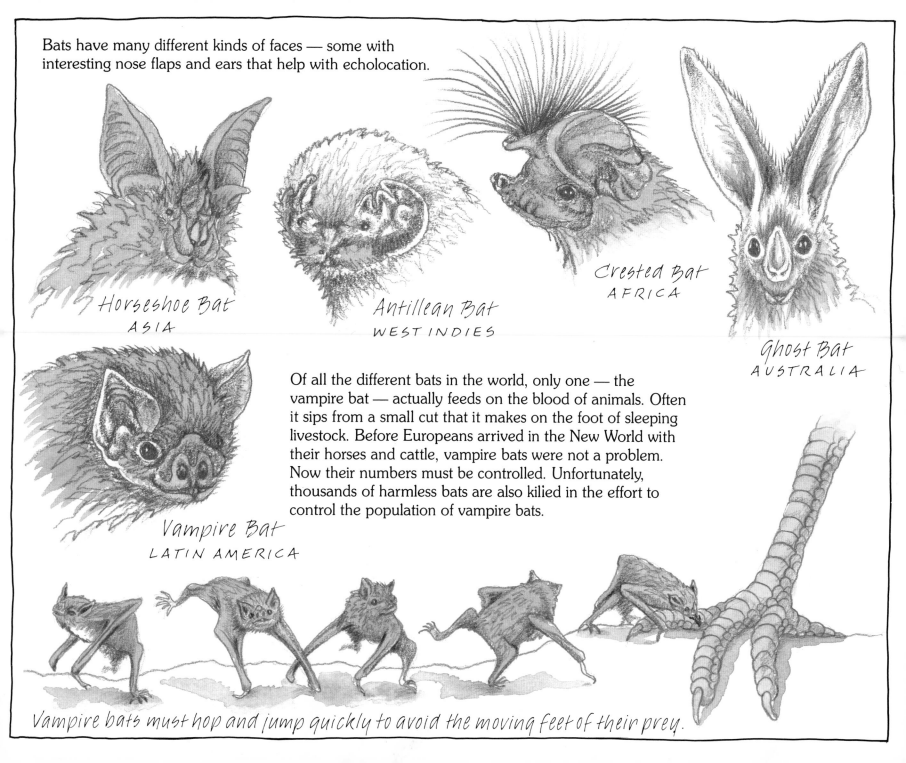

Bats have many different kinds of faces — some with interesting nose flaps and ears that help with echolocation.

Horseshoe Bat
ASIA

Antillean Bat
WEST INDIES

Crested Bat
AFRICA

Ghost Bat
AUSTRALIA

Of all the different bats in the world, only one — the vampire bat — actually feeds on the blood of animals. Often it sips from a small cut that it makes on the foot of sleeping livestock. Before Europeans arrived in the New World with their horses and cattle, vampire bats were not a problem. Now their numbers must be controlled. Unfortunately, thousands of harmless bats are also killed in the effort to control the population of vampire bats.

Vampire Bat
LATIN AMERICA

Vampire bats must hop and jump quickly to avoid the moving feet of their prey.

Besides inhabiting old buildings and caves, bats live in hollow trees, termite mounds, and animal burrows. They can also be found under bridges, rock ledges, palm leaves, and pieces of tree bark.

Tiny Honduran white bats roosting under a palm leaf

A long-nosed bat about to pollinate a saguaro cactus flower

If you would like to provide a home for a bat, you can install a bat box 10 to 15 feet up on a tree, facing the morning sun. The box should be open at the bottom, with vertical slats inside that are ½ to 1 inch apart.

SIDE VIEW

Things to Remember—

Only a tiny percentage of all bats carry rabies. Even so, you should never pick up a bat that is lying on the ground. It could be sick and, like any sick animal, might bite.

Never disturb hibernating bats. Losing the energy they would use to wake up and fly away from you could cause them to starve to death before spring.